MW00327136

Ninety Days

A collection of poems

Chyenne Daley

WRITERS REPUBLIC L.L.C.
515 Summit Ave. Unit R1
Union City, NJ 07087, USA

Website: *www.writersrepublic.com*
Hotline: *1-877-656-6838*
Email: *info@writersrepublic.com*

Ordering Information:
Quantity sales. Special discounts are available on quantity purchases by corporations, associations, and others. For details, contact the publisher at the address above.

Library of Congress Control Number:	2021931302	
ISBN-13:	978-1-64620-755-8	[Paperback Edition]
	978-1-64620-756-5	[Digital Edition]

Rev. date: 01/27/2021

For the women who get labeled as broken

whose hearts have depth for years

who have noticed the passing of time

does not decrease the love for him

it peeks up sporadically

it hides under your skin

between your finger nails

yearning to meet him once more

you are forever bonded by the pain

letting go was never easy

It's okay.

Table of Contents

Attraction

I nourished the thought that it was real

I mean after dealing with the worst you

sealed the deal

Your touch always soft and sweet

I longed for you

I thought we'd never meet

I remember when I saw those eyes

I knew they were for me

I declared you my own before you even got

the chance to know me

My mind saw our palms locked even after a

decade

but it was quickly dismissed

Protecting myself from such ideas was

essential despite the potential bliss

I could have eaten you up almost immediately

but I told myself to wait

You're broken but it's okay, let me fix you

I've always been good at that

I hear the bell on the door as we walk
inside
The sizzle of the grill shoots dopamine up
my spine
I smell the sweet mix of spices and marinated
meat
I hear the crunch of chips dipped in
guacamole
I see fresh corn tortillas
Mhm
Soft and hard
Pico de gallo
mhm
I want it all
My stomach smiles as we walk to our seat
Im tickled with joy
You know just what I like to eat

Date night

I want it all with you

I can see our future on your eye lids

I see dress fittings and photographers

Invitations and balloons

I see you and I jumping the broom

I fell in love with you almost immediately

All you had to do was look at me

You are perfect

You look like everything I prayed for

We fit so well

You are my glove

I snuggle inside your body

Inside your bones

Inside your skin

You are my home

My safe place

Where I wanna be when im not

Where I am even when im not there

I'm your shoulder

Your torso

Your rib

Your heart

I'll be apart of you forever

I let my heart pump its beats in your palm

Its safe there

I know no matter what you won't let it fall

Let it get a second off beat

Let it break

I just know

I trust you with my life

I wanna love on you with my words

I want you to taste them

Feel the letters crunch between your teeth

Pick the residue out with your tongue

Swallow it

Let them float in your esophagus

Run through your veins

Absorb its nutrients into your soul

Chyenne Daley

You are all I see

I only have eyes for you

You're like water

Essential

Fresh

Clean

Room temp

Just what I like to drink

When I'm with you I have tunnel vision

All that matters is you

With you there is no time

You eliminate the continued progress of

existence

There is no past or future

Just us

Right here

Right now

Chyenne Daley

You annoint my head with oil

My cups runs over

The mole on my nose is yours

The birth mark on the left side of my stomach

The wrinkles on my skin

The hyperpigmentation that lives on my nails

My face

My lips

The stretch marks on my backside

They belong to you

They tell you a story

They scream your name

They're preying on you

These curves

Yours

The chocolate that drips off my body

Sweet

Thick

Dark

You can do whatever you want with me

Have whatever you want from me

Intimacy

You didn't even have to touch me for my body
to invite you in
My mind already saw everything your fingers
wanted to do
The crevice of my legs had already began to
moisten
My body running hot
I could already taste you
White
Gooey
Lukewarm

Were sitting in the park

Its a nice cool night

Another date night

I feel the wind creep into my chest

I close my eyes wishing it was your breath

I watch as the trees sway in approval

Im staring at you

Your skin is glowing

You are so damn beautiful

We stop and sit on the bench

I read you some of my poems

I'm nervous but you seem impressed

You look me deep into my eyes

Im hoping my words are touching your soul

The small gestures of you

touching my face

kissing me

holding me

My favorite

Chyenne Daley

It was quiet as I waited for you

but the quiver of my vulva created

ripples through the silence

I indulge in thoughts of you

The anticipation overwhelmed my mind

Im done waiting

now's the time

Your tongue

Your delicate touch

My gasps

Loud

My heart races for more

Your hands are smooth as they grip my skin

I look back with a desire to see how deep

you are within

Your sweet licks makes me throb

I love it when you taste me

Sensual seduction marked by a sob

We stare at each other and begin to chuckle

Sharing so much passion as this brand new

couple

Chyenne Daley

Like my favorite meal on a sunday

it was you

Inside me

I can feel you growing in my stomach

I love the warmth of your body on mine

It's comforting

Safe

Peaceful

Even when asleep beside you I yearn more of

your flesh

I want to live inside your skin

Chyenne Daley

Compacted into one

Your manhood is as thick as my hair

You are density

Feeling you behind my throat brings me alive

slurping and sucking until you arrive

one hand partaking in movement as my mouth

does the rest

and I'm gagging on you in this orgasmic

quest

I can hear your heartbeat as I lay on your
chest
I close my eyes and concentrate as I try to
sync my beats with yours

You asked if you could suck the chocolate

off my skin

I froze

You said it wouldn't take long and that I

should sit still

I smiled and told you I taste extra sweet

you said I shouldn't worry

You love to eat

Bon appétit

Chyenne Daley

We could talk for days

Even when my eyes wanted sleep

my ears just wanted more of your words

My love is kind and strong

She'll travel miles just to hold your hand

My love is true and genuine like a newborn

baby who has just taken its first breath

There are no conditions to my love

You are safe here

I love you

Here take my heart

I give you access

To the deepest parts of me

Uncertainty

There was always red flags

There is always red flags

If you look close enough you'll see it

It's Always there

The question is will you believe it

Will you take it as a sign to proceed

Will you risk the danger

The potential scarring

The bruising

The rupture it may bring

Or will you follow the messages of your soul

Walk away without being told

The decision is in your hand

But remember to look closely

It's always there

If you look close enough

Red flags and green lights

Be careful

your mind plays tricks on you

just because you heard it doesn't mean it's

true

We make ourselves believe the things we

want it to

Chyenne Daley

I fell in love with your potential

that was my biggest mistake

Like the autumn leaves on a cold November
morning, you were there clinging to me like
tiny droplets of dew
I watched you fall from the sky so elegantly
as you always do
But today was different
I watched as the wind guided you astray
As you chuckled and enjoyed the ride away

you were always so sweet

A taste that lived on my tongue

Somehow overnight you've turned bitter

You make my lips push forward and my eyes

squint

I don't like the taste of you

I'm not well

My heart hurts

I can't think straight

Are you lying to me?

All I ever did was tell you the truth

I don't wanna talk about it

or think

or breath

I'm decompensating

Just let me be

I'm trying to get you off your pedestal

But you're too high

I can't reach you

I can feel the stretch in my arm as my body

extends forward

The tightening of my muscle as I reach

further and further

But there's no luck

Maybe try a ladder?

Okay this should help

I step up with eagerness in my eyes

Ok this should do it

1,2,3

Reach

Ugh

I let out a sigh as I feel the frustration

pushing through my pores

Why did I put you all the way up there

now I can't get you down

I'm kicking and screaming as I extend

Swaying my body as I reach to grab you

My palms are sweating and I'm losing my

patience

You're too high up

come down

Please

I shouldn't have put you up there

There was something about those eyes that
were erie
they said so much in the quiet of the night
When the world was asleep and my body numb
from your poison
they wandered
Like the greed of a balloon floating into the
vase blue sky
you searched for more
The quiet of the night couldn't satisfy you
nor could the appetite of my flesh

Do not dim your light to make his shine
Eventually he will leave you with nothing
but darkness

Chyenne Daley

You were way too broken for me to ever fix

There were so many disappointments

The subtle ones that I made excuses for

This taught you that I didnt value myself

and so you didn't either

If he's intimidated by you

It's a red flag

Blink twice so I know you're in danger

I'll stall while you pack your things up

You must leave and never return

You did not come to compete with his ego

Who knew that being with a strong woman

would frighten you

Scare you to death

Rip you to shreds

You are never too dominant

The problem is that he is weak

When he makes you question

If its you or him

Choose the latter

Betrayal

It's raining today

you always said the rain meant a change was
near

I guess you always knew the future

I didn't agree to share you with her

there was never any consent

An unwarranted act

I am shackled with despair

Even with me living in your skin it wouldn't

have stopped you from deceiving me

cheating on me

lying to me

It's so innate for you to manipulate

Second nature

A fixed part of who you are

An uncontrollable urge

I am afraid of you

I watched as my body rejected food

As I laid in bed as still as a rock

Empty with nothing but my tears for comfort

I watched as I had my first panic attack

As my body fought to keep it all down but

inevitably throw up in devastation

My stomachs in knots

I'm sick

Sick to my stomach

Running to the toliet to spill out more

of you

I watched as my mind fluttered to make sense

of my reality

I don't understand

I watched as I walked outside with no

direction

My body so weak that I went with the wind

I watched the days go by without sleep

My eyes carrying the weight of our union

I watched as the pills in my palm flew into

my mouth

I just need quiet

I watched my tears go from soft cries to

loud sobs

My face numb

My body running with chills

I am hurting

Suddenly like the smoke clearing after

a fire I had clarity

like the sudden shattered of a glass

I was blindsided

shocked

debilitated

this was a game I did not agree to be a

part

of yet felt so firmly placed

I realize now that only the thought of you

was mine

The thought of us growing overtime

A facade too lovely to forget and too

connected to detach

I wondered where the broken pieces of my

heart

belonged and I struggled to get them back

I am the sweetest person I know

The most thoughtful

caring

understanding little human being

A delicate flower

A diamond

A giver

A lover

All I ever did was honor you

Praise you

Love you

And look what you did to me

I showered you with wisdom

Submerged you in my parents teachings

Fed you with knowledge

Heightened your reality

Took you out of the box you were firmly

placed in

Opened your eyes to life

Love

Luxury

Endorsed your body with rose water and

scriptures

Incense and sage

With candles that lit you up

I honored you

Showed you what it felt like to be a king

To reap the benefits of being with a black

queen

Imparted the language of adventure into

your being

I poured my all into you

Gave you life

But you tried to take life from me

You said you're not a monster then who

are you?

Your fingers cut like knives

You ooze deception with a smile

Your scent is unforgettable

potent

and you come prepared to play

But your appearance doesn't frighten me

you're a monster in disguise

When you're ready you salivate on my chest

then clean me up when you're done

You take but you don't give

you hurt but you don't heal

Who else would cause such harm unprovoked?

You showed me evil lives in the ones you
trust
The ones you would do anything for
Your evil is intoxicating

Thick and contagious

It's beginning to cloud my mind and soul
I'm becoming dark and ominous
I live in hatred

I'm reading books about forgiveness and
 practicing peace

They say my heart turned rigid

They dare me to soften it

They say it's brave

They say it's courageous

But I don't want to

You tried to break me

Distorted my reality

I'm having disorganized thoughts

Delusions that make it hard to breath

Floridly psychotic

Who am I?

I want to stay rigid, this place is my new
 home

I'll see you again in my mind someday

tomorrow or the next

Then maybe we can get even

when I light flames to your chest

You taught me betrayal

thank you.

When you left I'm sure you thought I'd

chase you

Fall to your feet and beg you to stay

Pop up at your job

Wait for you outside

Call you repeatedly

Sit at your doorstep with watery eyes

Stop living

Stop breathing

Dig myself into a hole

Stop attending work

Lose focus of my dreams

Rip my skin off and give you what was left

of me

Yeah I thought so too.

I dare you to seek the help you need

To do the work

To hold space for yourself

To take accountability

To sit with the shame of who you are

To feel every broken piece of you

I dare you to love yourself enough to pick

through your flesh

To really examine your behaviors

To get to the root of who you are

To find purpose

I dare you to dig

Beneath your skin

Beneath your bones

Dig deep within

Search through your body

Feel the bone marrow

The sticky paste of your mucus

The density of your intestines

Learn how it works

Chyenne Daley

What it takes in

Let the acid of your stomach burn your

fingertips as you continue to dig

Facing your darkest secrets

Your deepest fears

Your biggest regrets

The things only you know

The things you would never say out loud

Then sit with it

Let the poison plummet from your feces

Release the parts of yourself that keep you

in bondage

Give yourself holistic care

Only then can you truly be the good person

you always thought you were

Nostalgia

Your pillow soft lips alone

could soften the effect of an impact

And so I lay here wishing you could

save me from this wreck

Chyenne Daley

You are perfect

You look so good with your mask on

You are so good at lying

So good at pretending to be a good guy

So good at making me feel like the only girl

you wanted

So good at playing victim

At blaming

So good at never taking accountability

At being sneaky

At hiding your true intentions

You were so good at masking you you are

So many things can happen in ninety days

People fall in love

Close a deal on a new home

Study hard then pass an exam

Travel to new countries

Study abroad

Buy a new car

Meet new friends

Become an extrovert

Finish the first trimester of pregnancy

Gain a desired weight

Lose a desired weight

Become an entrepreneur

Make a larger salary

Accomplish a new goal

Join a book club

But in ninety days you chose to ruin my

world

Was it hard laying your body down with
someone else
Knowing I had no clue
Knowing all I ever wanted was you
Transferring energies and fluids with an
imposter
Releasing your toxins into the bodies of
living breathing beings
Whispering stories in my ears
The good ones that you knew I would believe
Licking the crumbs off your lips as you fed
me more lies
Did it ever become exhausting
Did you ever want to stop
Ever think about your actions?

I'm repulsed
You disgust me

Who knew the memory of my poems

would be the only thing left of you

You use to wash my hair

Give me massages

Lotion my body

Hold my hand during car rides

Hug me

Kiss me

I was safe then

I was yours then

Of course you didn't value me

you don't even value yourself

Sometimes I type your number in the

message box

It comes up green

Guess you still have me blocked

I guess you'll never face what you've done

Was it worth it?

Was it really that fun?

Unanswered questions

You always told me that I shouldn't stand

while I eat, remember?

I still do that

I wonder if you still lie and cheat

Babe

I miss you

Come over

You're beautiful

I'll call you soon

Facetime me

Sit next to me

Shower with me

No, you hang up first

Can I lotion your body

I love you

Im still trying to get you out my system

I've taken all sorts of western medicine

I've tried sweating you out my pores

Even took pills to quiet the noise

Im exhausting my immune system

my body

my mind

But you're still here

lingering in my spirit

Please

Just go away

I'm so tired of fighting you

Tonight I no longer despise you

I know its short lived but I stay here

Breathing it in deep into my lungs

Replaying our talks

Our laughs

We were always so fun

I miss the silly voices we made as we spoke

our lovers language

And I can still smell the beef on the stove

Burgers

Mhm

I breath this in too

Soaking in the blissfulness before breathing

in you

I miss you

I hate you

I miss you

I hate you

How funny is it that I tried to force the
pieces

Tried to twist and bend into shapes

Molding myself into squares and circles of
a mundane view

We were never the same

You chose a rock when you had a diamond

you never knew what was good for you

If only she knew that you still

think about me as you undress her

as you hold her hands

As you whisper in her ear

If only we had magical powers

If only we could read minds

Then you would have no one left to fool

Please

Never in your life make the

mistake of comparing me to another woman

there is no competition

I vibrate too high

My energy is too unique

Too expansive

Too liberating

We will never vibrate on the same frequency

I know you may not think so now

But I promise you I'll be your biggest regret

Chyenne Daley

You will try to find pieces of me

in every woman you meet and

you will be disappointed every time

Today is day 105 since you've been gone

I wish my heart understood that it was time

to move on

I wish the thought of you didn't hurt so bad

And seeing your face didn't make me so sad

Like a bandage to a cold sore I must

conceal you

I want to heal, but what if I never do?

I miss you

Healing

Longing for the person who dismissed me

Rejected me

Hurt me

It's okay...

Healing is layered

Chyenne Daley

Who would have thought that the

very thing I wanted so badly I would learn

to despise

Loving you and mourning you felt

so good as they happened simultaneously

I can see the silhouette of the train on the
grey cold bricks as it moves with the world
I look up with deep curiosity in my eyes and
see the cloudy white mist of the moon
I hear the horn of the train blow loudly,
and watch the sway of my legs as the speed
deepens into the abyss
I think of you in this movement
I can see us in the clouds and in the
reflection of the moon
I try to hold onto the last part of us but
the train continues to proceed
It passes the trees that were once our love
the buildings of our memories
and the bridge that connected our souls.

As I ride on I can see the river beneath me
and I watch as the waves crash against one
another
I'm reminded of you again

the water somehow represents the copious
amounts of tears I shed
But the train is still moving at full speed
there's no catching up to the past
it has already gone
Leaving you behind along with the changing
autumn leaves
My destination is near and it's time for me
to go
I sit back and ground myself in the gratitude
of being able to love
Loving me enough for the both of us when
you choose yourself Loving me enough to let
you go
I hear it again
the horn of the train
it blows once more and I realize this is it
I close my eyes as reality starts to hit

Self validation has to start with the truth

I miss you

I have no shame in that

I give myself compassion and understanding -

the gift of honesty

I understand why I landed here

I slowly unpack as I begin to let you go

I am no longer afraid of the silence

I sit alone with my thoughts on

the edge of my comfy red sofa

I hold my knees close to my chest

Wrap my blanket around my body

And cradle them

My happiness was never contingent on you

Everyone keeps saying time heals

but it's a lie

You chewed me up and spit me out right here

on this coarse concrete

Your saliva still leaves its mark deep

beneath the ground

Time has done nothing

I realize now that you were blind

with eyes that glistened without command

and a smile that yearned for approval

you were always broken

But I saw something in you

I loved the parts of you that you weren't

yet able to see

heard thoughts you weren't yet able to hear

I saw the depth in you

the parts of you that were lost until you

found me

But blind you were

Blinded by these very parts of yourself

They prohibited you from seeing beyond what

eyes could see

beyond your inner child and fears

they prohibited you from loving me

For the women who get labeled as broken

whose hearts have depth for years

Who have noticed the passing of time does

not decrease the love for him

It peeks up sporadically

It hides under your skin

between your finger nails

yearning to meet him once more

You are forever bonded by the pain

letting go was never easy.

It's okay.

Shaking the dust off my feet before I proceed

making sure to get every piece of residue

that you intended to stay on me

The bitterness, anger, and rejection can no

longer live here it's time for you to go

Return to sender, you have no place in my

home

Chyenne Daley

I wrote myself a love letter today

You didn't cross my mind at all

I look up and smile

today will be a good day

How dare you make me feel inadequate

when my adequacy stretches far beyond your

conscious mind

Far beyond the physical realm

Beyond your wildest dreams

How dare you

For many days I carried you on my back

I carried your guilt and shame

It was heavy

But I held on

I gained blisters and sores that inflamed

my skin

Shifted bones and tore muscles as I carried

the weight

But today I give it back to you

The mind is interesting

You're beginning to feel like a creature of

my imagination

A distant memory

I'm no longer able to feel you or

Hold you

Are you even real?

Sometimes I'm not sure

I check by looking at photos of us

We had our own little world didn't we

I let my body exude with fluids as I yearn

who you were

My heart flutters as I panic

My eyes burn as I cry

My head spins

My heart hurts

That's when I know you were real

At some point I won't even remember you

I'll have a life better than yours

I'll have children

A husband

Purpose

Substance

Happiness

I'll look back and laugh

I'll be clear of you

You'll no longer live in my sinuses

I'll be able to breath

Inhaling the life I've always wanted

I'll be able to smile with teeth of resilience

But for now I understand that you occupy my

left atrium

I can feel you picking away at the tissue

I'm making peace with this

It's temporary

Everything about you is temporary

Dear Sleep,

You don't know how much I've missed you
I prayed for the noise in my head to quiet
down
I waited countless days for your return
Thank you for coming back to me

You are a divine being

An angel

The most precious person you know

You're delicate

And kind

And funny

And loving

You are resilient

You stand on the shoulders of your ancestors

They fought battles

Wore scars of victory

You share their blood

You are strong

You are resilient

Remember

Gratitudes

I am grateful for life

I am grateful for healing

For learning

For growth

I am grateful for the songs by

Chronixx that always get me through

I'm grateful for morning affirmations

and guided meditations

For manicures and eyelash appointments

I am grateful for God

For the sermons I watched for hours

For the poets who inspired me

The podcasts that fed my soul

I'm grateful for my therapist

For the tears that released a

little more pain each day

for my friends and family who held space

For my journal whose pages were

strong enough to hold my agony

For the ones Who read drafts of my poems

I am grateful for your constant enthusiasm

For my busy work schedule that

kept my mind occupied

I am grateful for the gift of writing

for turning my pain into art

I'm grateful for every reader

Thank you for being apart of my world

Thank you for holding space for my truth

CPSIA information can be obtained
at www.ICGtesting.com
Printed in the USA
BVHW071050110321
602311BV00003B/223

9 781646 207558